WE'RE ON YOUR SIDE, CHARLIE BROWN

Selected Cartoons From

BUT WE LOVE YOU,
CHARLIE BROWN
Vol. I

by Charles M. Schulz

A FAWCETT CREST BOOK
FAWCETT PUBLICATIONS, INC., GREENWICH, CONN.
MEMBER OF AMERICAN BOOK PUBLISHERS COUNCIL, INC.

Other Peanuts Books in Fawcett Crest Editions:

D1147 YOU'RE MY HERO, CHARLIE BROWN!
D1097 WHO DO YOU THINK YOU ARE, CHARLIE BROWN?
D1070 GOOD OL' SNOOPY
D1134 YOU ARE TOO MUCH, CHARLIE BROWN
D1142 VERY FUNNY, CHARLIE BROWN
D1141 FOR THE LOVE OF PEANUTS!
D1140 WHAT NEXT, CHARLIE BROWN?
D1133 FUN WITH PEANUTS
D1130 YOU'RE A WINNER, CHARLIE BROWN!
D1129 GOOD GRIEF, CHARLIE BROWN!
D1128 HEY, PEANUTS!
D1115 THE WONDERFUL WORLD OF PEANUTS
D1113 HERE COMES CHARLIE BROWN!
D1099 HERE COMES SNOOPY
D1096 LET'S FACE IT, CHARLIE BROWN
D1164 THIS IS YOUR LIFE, CHARLIE BROWN!

Only 50¢ Each—Wherever Paperbacks Are Sold

If your dealer is sold out, send only cover price plus 10¢ each for postage and handling to Crest Books, Fawcett Publications, Inc., Greenwich, Connecticut 06830. Please order by number and title. If five or more books are ordered, no postage or handling charge is necessary. No Canadian orders. Catalog available on request.

This book, prepared especially for Fawcett Publications, Inc., comprises the first half of BUT WE LOVE YOU, CHARLIE BROWN, and is reprinted by arrangement with Holt, Rinehart and Winston, Inc.

Thirteenth Fawcett Crest printing, September 1968

Published by Fawcett World Library,
67 West 44th Street, New York, N.Y. 10036
Printed in the United States of America

PLINK!
?
PLINK!
PLINK!
PLINK!
GOOD GRIEF!
PLINK PLINK
PLINK
PLINK
PLINK PLINK
THIS POCKET LEAKS!
SCHULZ

I WISH I COULD BE SOMEBODY'S FRIEND..
I'D EVEN BE GLAD TO BE A FRIEND IN NEED..

INDEED?
SCHULZ

THIS SHOULD BE A WONDERFUL SUMMER IF I EVER LIVE THROUGH SPRING!
SCHULZ

GOOD GRIEF!!
WHOEVER INVENTED ROLLER-SKATES MUST HAVE HATED LITTLE GIRLS!
SCHULZ

HI "PIG-PEN".. WHAT ARE YOU DOING?
NOTHING... I JUST LIKE TO SIT HERE AND WATCH THE REST OF THE WORLD GO BY
UH HUH ..
IT LOOKS LIKE A LOT OF IT HAS STAYED WITH YOU!
SCHULZ

LUCY, WHY IS THE SKY BLUE?
BECAUSE IT ISN'T GREEN!!
THAT JUST SHOWS HOW STUPID I AM... I THOUGHT THERE WOULD BE A MORE COMPLICATED REASON...
SCHULZ

LOOK, SCHROEDER..
I FOUND YOU A
NEW BUST OF
BEETHOVEN!
THIS ISN'T BEETHOVEN..THIS
IS GEORGE WASHINGTON!
IT
IS?
WELL, I'LL BE!
I NEVER COULD TELL ONE
COMPOSER FROM THE OTHER!
SCHULZ

LOOK, SCHROEDER..
I FOUND ANOTHER
STATUE OF
BEETHOVEN..
THIS ISN'T BEETHOVEN! THIS IS
GEORGE WASHINGTON AGAIN!
WELL, I'LL BE! THEY SURE
LOOK A LOT ALIKE...
DO YOU SUPPOSE THEY
COULD HAVE BEEN RELATED?
SCHULZ

I'LL BET I WOULD HAVE MADE A GOOD BALD EAGLE!
SCHULZ

I'M SCARED TO PLAY ANY MORE, CHARLIE BROWN..
THERE'S A VULTURE SITTING ON THE CROQUET STAKE..
A VULTURE?
OH, GOOD GRIEF!
SCHULZ

DO YOU KNOW ANYTHING ABOUT VULTURES, CHARLIE BROWN?
ALL I KNOW IS THAT THEY'RE VERY FIERCE-LOOKING..
I THINK THAT DOG IS LOSING HIS MIND!
SCHULZ

GET OUT OF HERE!!
SCHULZ

DO VULTURES FLY VERY HIGH, CHARLIE BROWN?
OH, YES...USUALLY THEY CIRCLE IN THE AIR..THEY GO AROUND AND AROUND...
SUDDENLY, WITH A GREAT FLURRY OF WINGS, THEY DROP TO THE GROUND!

WUMP!
SCHULZ

RATS! A REAL VULTURE WOULD NEVER LET HIMSELF BE STARED DOWN!
SCHULZ

I FOUND A WORM, BUT I'M GOING TO PUT HIM BACK..
FOR ALL I KNOW HE MAY BE A VERY IMPORTANT WORM..
I WOULDN'T WANT TO DEPRIVE ANY GROUP OF ITS LEADER..
SCHULZ

HE'S DOING PRETTY WELL, I THINK..
WHO'S DOING PRETTY WELL?
LINUS...HE'S LEARNING TO DRESS HIMSELF..

OF COURSE, ON SOME DAYS HE DOES BETTER THAN ON OTHERS
SCHULZ

?
"I LIKE LUDWIG"
I MIGHT HAVE KNOWN!
SCHULZ

THERE'S SOMETHING ABOUT THAT BLANKET THAT ANNOYS ME!
SCHULZ
WHY NOT TRY LOOKING UPON IT AS A CONVERSATION PIECE?

MY DAD HAS A BETTER UNDERSTANDING OF FOREIGN POLICY THAN YOUR DAD..
SCHULZ
OH, GOOD GRIEF!

I WONDER IF BEETHOVEN WOULD HAVE LIKED ME?
OH, I'M SURE HE WOULD HAVE LIKED YOU, SCHROEDER...
HE DIDN'T LIKE VERY MANY PEOPLE, YOU KNOW..
DO YOU REALLY THINK SO?
SURE
BUT I'LL BET HE WOULD HAVE LIKED ME EVEN BETTER!
SCHULZ

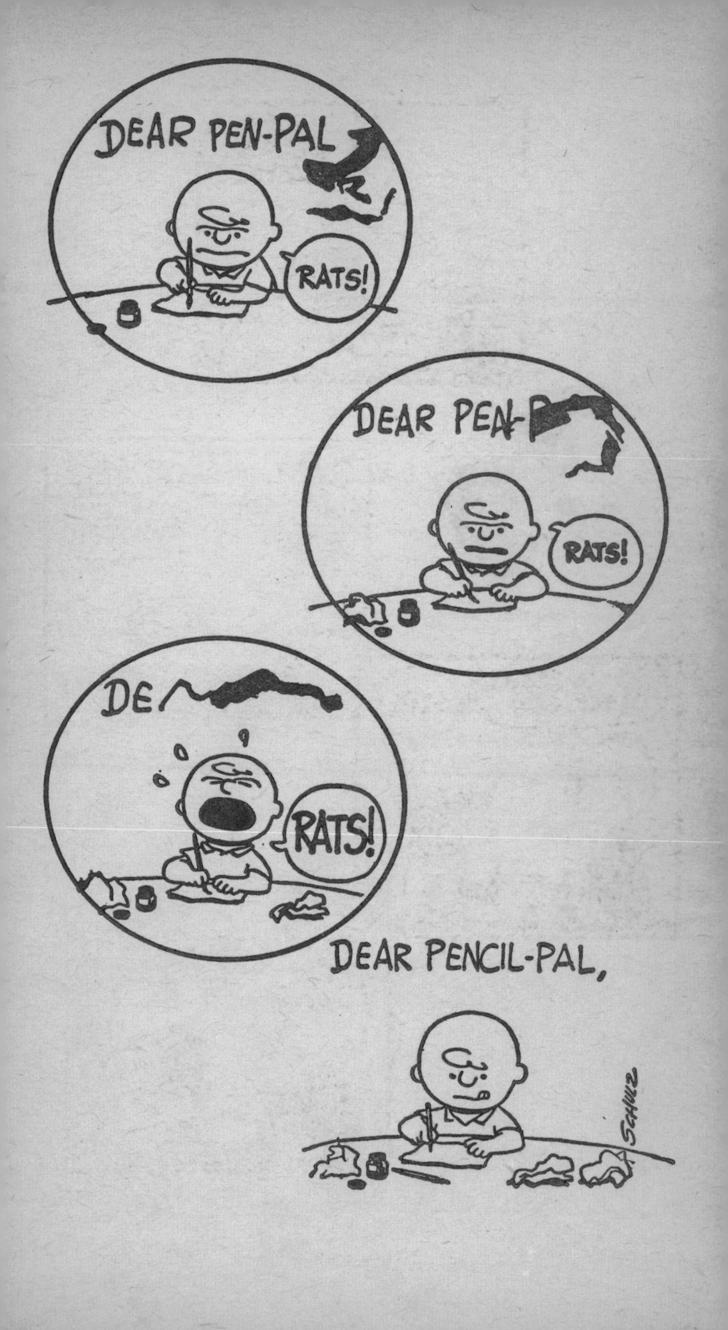
DEAR PEN-PAL
RATS!
DEAR PEN-P
RATS!
DE
RATS!
DEAR PENCIL-PAL,
SCHULZ

DEAR PENCIL-PAL:
I KNOW YOU ARE REALLY MY PEN-PAL, BUT I AM GOING TO HAVE TO CALL YOU MY PENCIL-PAL.
THIS IS BECAUSE I DO NOT PRINT WELL WITH A PEN.
HOPING YOU WILL NOT BE OFFENDED, I REMAIN YOURS TRULY, CHARLIE BROWN

WHAT DO YOU AND THIS PENCIL-PAL OF YOURS WRITE ABOUT?
OH, HE TELLS ME ABOUT HIS COUNTRY, AND I TELL HIM ABOUT OURS...
U.S.
YOU SOUND LIKE A COUPLE OF SPIES TO ME!
SCHULZ

WHAT'S THAT, CHARLIE BROWN?
THIS IS A LETTER TO MY PENCIL-PAL ..
OF COURSE, HE'S REALLY A PEN-PAL. BUT I CALL HIM A PENCIL-PAL BECAUSE I CAN'T WRITE WITH A PEN.
THAT SOUNDS LOGICAL..
DO YOU SUPPOSE THERE ARE ANY CRAYON-PALS AROUND?
SCHULZ

DEAR PENCIL-PAL,
YOU ARE MY ONLY FRIEND. NOT COUNTING YOU I AM FRIENDLESS. I HAVE NO OTHER FRIENDS.
YOUR FRIEND, CHARLIE BROWN
P.S. EVERYBODY HATES ME
SCHULZ

HOW LONG DO YOU THINK IT WILL TAKE FOR YOUR LETTER TO GET TO YOUR PENCIL-PAL?
I DON'T KNOW.. A FEW DAYS I SUPPOSE..
WHAT KIND OF STAMP DID YOU PUT ON IT?
STAMP?
SCHULZ

STOMP!
I THOUGHT YOUR MOTTO WAS 'LIVE AND LET LIVE'?
HE WASN'T REALLY LIVING!
SCHULZ

WAAH!
PLEASE DON'T CRY.. LUCY..
WADDYA MEAN, DON'T CRY?!!
WHY SHOULD I DEPRIVE MYSELF OF AN EMOTIONAL OUTLET?!
SCHULZ

GEE, IT SEEMS LIKE A LONG TIME SINCE I WAS A PUPPY...
I REMEMBER THAT FIRST NIGHT WHEN THEY BROUGHT ME HOME...
SNOOPY
THEY PUT A CLOCK IN MY BED TO KEEP ME COMPANY...I GUESS ITS TICKING WAS SUPPOSED TO SOOTHE ME..
SNOOPY
IT SURE SOOTHED ME ALL RIGHT...WHEN THAT ALARM WENT OFF, I ALMOST HIT THE CEILING!
SCHULZ

WHEN I WAS A PUPPY, EVERY DAY WAS A HAPPY DAY..
THE SUN USED TO SHINE IN THE MORNING, AND ALL OF THE EVENINGS WERE COOL AND PLEASANT..
SUDDENLY... BANG!
..AND I'M IN MY DECLINING YEARS!
SCHULZ

YOU HAVE TO KNOW A LOT OF THINGS BEFORE YOU CAN ENTER KINDER-GARTEN, LINUS..
YOU HAVE TO BE ABLE TO USE A HANDKERCHIEF, GET A DRINK OF WATER ALONE, PUT ON YOUR OWN COAT AND CUT WITH SCISSORS!
WOW!
I NEVER REALIZED THE REQUIREMENTS WERE SO RIGID!
SCHULZ

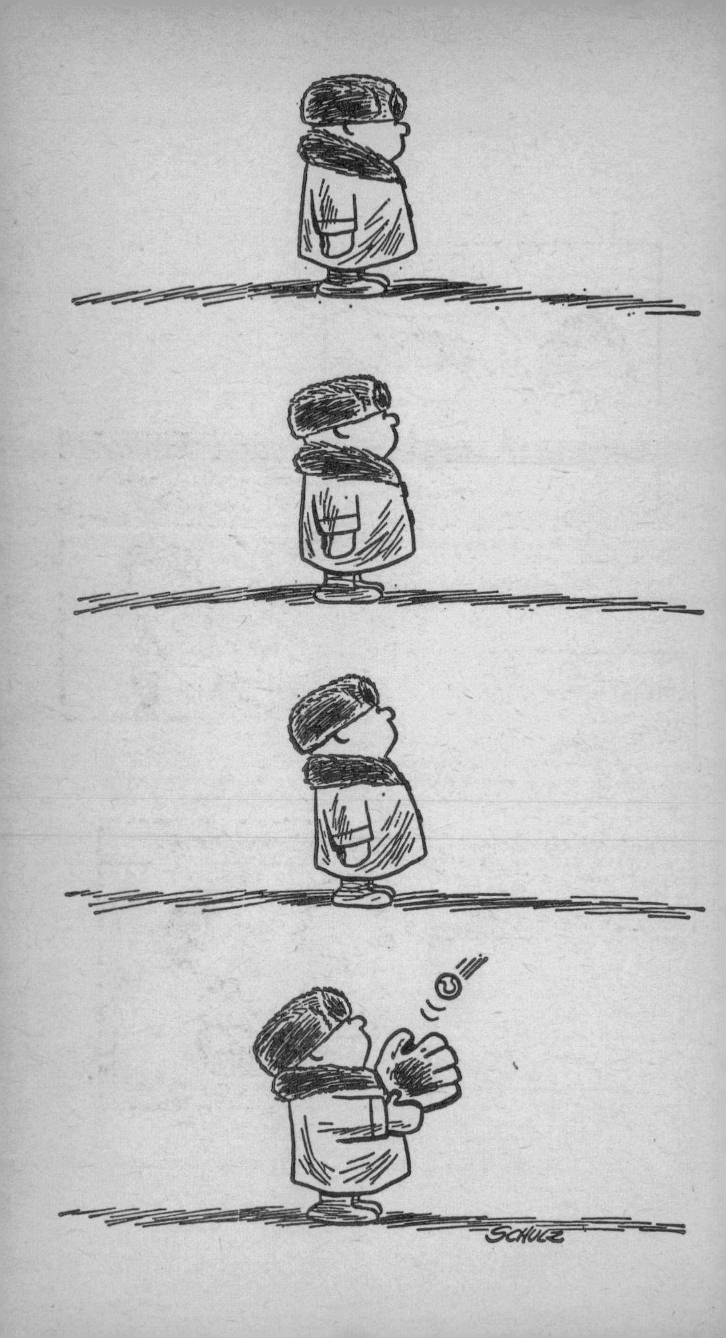
SCHULZ

THE EARTH IS OVER-POPULATED!
FAMILIES ARE GETTING TOO BIG! THERE ARE TOO MANY BABIES BEING BORN!
THE EARTH CAN'T FEED THIS MANY PEOPLE!
WHY DON'T YOU LEAVE?
SCHULZ

I'M A GREAT BELIEVER IN EDUCATION..
I INTEND TO BE THE MOST EDUCATED PERSON IN THIS PART OF THE CITY..
I INTEND TO BE THE MOST EDUCATED PERSON IN THE WHOLE WORLD..

I'LL NEVER BE SATISFIED UNTIL I'M TOO SMART FOR MY OWN GOOD!
SCHULZ

?
HERE, VIOLET..
THESE ARE FOR
YOU BECAUSE I
LIKE YOU...
WHY, HOW NICE! THANK YOU,
LINUS...THANK YOU VERY MUCH
WHAT DID HE GIVE YOU?
SOME FRENCH-FRIES WITH A
RUBBER BAND AROUND THEM!
SCHULZ

HI, CHARLIE BROWN..
HI, "PIG-PEN"
THAT'S THE ONLY KID I KNOW WHO CAN RAISE A CLOUD OF DUST WALKING IN THE RAIN!
SCHULZ

ALL RIGHT LET'S CUT OUT THE CLOWNING!
YOU'LL NEVER CATCH A BALL THAT WAY..
CLUMP!
SCHULZ

NOBODY BREAKS HIM UP LIKE STEPHEN FOSTER!
SCHULZ

HELLO, CHARLIE BROWN..
THIS IS MY NEW HI-FI PARASOL..
IT'S VERY PRETTY
HOW CAN A PARASOL BE HI-FI?
SCHULZ

GOOD HOT DOGS, HUH, CHARLIE BROWN?
FAIR, I GUESS...
A HOT DOG JUST DOESN'T TASTE RIGHT WITHOUT A BALL GAME IN FRONT OF IT..
SCHULZ

SCHULZ

WELL, I WARNED HIM!
HE'S BEEN TAGGING AFTER ME ALL MORNING! EVERY TIME I'D TURN AROUND, THERE HE'D BE!
I COULDN'T STAND IT ANY LONGER...
SCHULZ

LUCY, WHAT'S THE DIFFERENCE BETWEEN A BUG AND AN INSECT?
WELL, PHYSICALLY THERE'S NO DIFFERENCE AT ALL..IT'S MOSTLY A MATTER OF CLASS DISTINCTION.. YOU KNOW...BIRTH, BREEDING... THAT SORT OF THING..
I SURE ENVY YOU YOUR KNOWLEDGE OF NATURE..

LOOK AT THIS BUG, LINUS..
LOOK AT THE EXPRESSION ON HIS FACE..
HE MUST BE A PRETTY SMART BUG...

HE'S GRINNING SORT OF KNOWINGLY!
SCHULZ

BUGS ARE SO FASCINATING..
Z
OH, OH! A BIG BLACK BEETLE!
?
STEP ON IT!
I MUST HAVE GOT HIM..
SCHULZ

YOU KNOW WHAT I THINK?
I THINK THIS WOULD BE A BETTER WORLD IF THERE WERE MORE UNDERSTANDING BETWEEN PEOPLE AND BUGS..
MAYBE IF WE TRIED TO UNDERSTAND THEM, WE COULD EVEN LEARN TO APPRECIATE THEM...

WHY DON'T THEY TRY TO UNDERSTAND **US**?
SCHULZ

YOU'RE SO WORRIED ABOUT TRYING TO UNDERSTAND THOSE STUPID BUGS..
WHY DON'T YOU TRY TO UNDERSTAND ME? I'M YOUR BROTHER! AREN'T I WORTH MORE THAN A BUG?!!
SCHULZ
I SHOULD KNOW BETTER THAN TO ASK THINGS LIKE THAT.

HI, THERE!
YOU SURE ARE A CUTE LITTLE BUG
SCHULZ
BUT WHAT A COLD NOSE!

SCHROEDER, WHY IS IT YOU LIKE BEETHOVEN BETTER THAN YOU LIKE ME?
BEETHOVEN WAS BEETHOVEN AND YOU ARE YOU!
THAT DOESN'T EVEN LEAVE ROOM FOR DISCUSSION...
SCHULZ

I'M SORRY I HURT YOUR FEELINGS, CHARLIE BROWN..
WHY DON'T YOU CALL **ME** WHAT I CALLED **YOU**? THEN WE'LL BE EVEN!
NO, I COULD NEVER DO THAT... NO, I JUST COULDN'T... NO, I'M SURE I COULD NEVER DO THAT...
BUT **WHY NOT**?
I FORGOT WHAT IT WAS YOU CALLED ME..
SCHULZ

"AS SOON AS THE WEATHER BECOMES WARM, ANIMALS COME OUT FROM THEIR WINTER HIDING PLACES.."
"THEY LIKE TO FIND A WARM PLACE IN THE SUN WHERE THEY CAN SLEEP.."
"OFTEN YOU CAN SEE THEM DOZING PEACEFULLY ON A ROCK.."
Z
SCHULZ

"ANIMALS FEEL THE COMING OF SPRING IN MUCH THE SAME WAY THAT HUMANS DO..."
"SOMEHOW THEY SENSE THE FEELING OF NEWNESS OF LIFE WHICH SPRING HAS TO OFFER."
"DURING THIS TIME OF YEAR IT IS NOT UNUSUAL TO SEE AN ANIMAL BOUNDING GAILY THROUGH THE UNDERBRUSH"
SCHULZ

"FOR ANIMALS SPRING IS THE BEST TIME OF THE YEAR.."
"SPRING RELEASES THEM FROM THE CONFINEMENT OF WINTER.."
"..AND IT BRINGS TO THEM, AS IT BRINGS TO US, A WONDERFUL FEELING OF WELL-BEING!"
SCHULZ

BONK
WHEW
YOU BLOCKHEAD!
?
SCHULZ
I JUST CAN'T RESIST ADDING INSULT TO INJURY..

LUCY, HOW MUCH IS SIX FROM FOUR?
SIX FROM FOUR?! YOU CAN'T SUBTRACT SIX FROM FOUR..
YOU CAN'T SUBTRACT A BIGGER NUMBER FROM A SMALLER NUMBER
YOU CAN IF YOU'RE STUPID!
SCHULZ

DEAR?PENCIL-PAL?
HOW?ARE? YOU?
DOING?IN?SCHOOL?
WE?LEARN?
SOMETHING?NEW?
EVERY? DAY?
TODAY?WE?LEARNED?
HOW?TO?MAKE?
QUESTION?MARKS?
SCHULZ

DEAR PENCIL-PAL,
HOW HAVE YOU BEEN?
RATS! WHAT I NEED IS SOME STATIONERY WITH **LINES** ON IT!
DEAR PENCIL-PAL,
HOW HAVE YOU BEEN?
SCHULZ

THERE GOES CHARLIE BROWN MAILING ANOTHER LETTER TO HIS PENCIL-PAL..
I KIND OF WISH I HAD A PENCIL-PAL...OF COURSE, I CAN'T WRITE ANYWAY..
ALL I COULD EVER DO IS MAKE A PAW PRINT..

THAT'S JUST WHAT I NEED...A PAW PRINT-PAL!
SCHULZ

YOU KNOW, I WOULDN'T BE SURPRISED IF THOSE TWO GOT MARRIED SOMEDAY..
THEY'RE REALLY TWO OF A KIND..
SHE LIKES HORSES, AND HE DOESN'T!
SCHULZ

SCHROEDER, IF THE TIME EVER CAME THAT YOU HAD TO CHOOSE BETWEEN ME AND THIS PIANO, WHAT WOULD YOU DO?
I'D LOOK YOU RIGHT IN THE EYE, AND I'D SAY, "I'LL TAKE THE PIANO!"
SCHULZ
STUPID PIANO!

"PIG-PEN" NEVER SAYS VERY MUCH, DOES HE?
HE'S AFRAID TO...WHENEVER HE TALKS, THE DIRT ON HIS FACE FLAKES OFF, AND FALLS ON THE GROUND BY HIS FEET.
THAT'S NOT TRUE!!
SCHULZ

CHARLIE BROWN, WHAT WOULD YOU DO IF YOU WERE SUDDENLY CALLED INTO THE ARMY?
HOW SHOULD I KNOW?
WELL, DON'T YOU WORRY ABOUT IT?
OF COURSE NOT!

HOW COME YOU NEVER WORRY ABOUT THINGS LIKE THAT?
SCHULZ

WHY AREN'T YOU IN THE ARMY, CHARLIE BROWN?
BECAUSE I'M TOO YOUNG, THAT'S WHY! BOY, YOU SURE CAN ASK SOME STUPID QUESTIONS...
ARE YOU **SURE** THAT'S THE REASON? ARE YOU **SURE**? HUH? **ARE** YOU? **HUH?**
ARE YOU SURE YOU'RE JUST NOT A LITTLE BIT **SCARED**? HUH? HUH?
OH, GOOD GRIEF...
SCHULZ

SLACKER!!!

ISN'T SPRING WONDERFUL, LINUS?
THE TREES, THE SHRUBS THE GRASS..
EVERYTHING IS TURNING GREEN...
WHAT IF YOU DON'T **LIKE** GREEN?
SCHULZ

YOU'RE ALWAYS TALKING ABOUT SPRING! WELL, I HATE SPRING!
NOW, WE'LL NEVER HAVE ANY MORE SNOW! HERE I AM, ONLY FOUR YEARS OLD, AND I'LL NEVER SEE SNOW AGAIN!!
WHAT ABOUT NEXT WINTER?! THERE'LL BE ANOTHER WINTER YOU KNOW!
THERE. WILL? GEE, I DIDN'T KNOW THAT...
I THOUGHT IT WAS SORT OF A ONE-SHOT DEAL!
SCHULZ

SIGH

SCHULZ

BOY, HOW THAT GIRL CAN TALK!
TALK TALK TALK TALK
TALK TALK TALK TALK

SOME DAYS SHE SOUNDS AS IF SHE WERE RECORDED AT '33⅓' AND PLAYED AT '78'!
SCHULZ

WHAT DO YOU HAVE THERE, LUCY?
NOTHING... JUST A RECORD... JUST A NEW RECORD...
WELL, COME ON...LET ME SEE IT..
"MUSIC TO FUSS BY"
SCHULZ

MY GRAMPA SAYS THAT WHEN HE WAS LITTLE, KIDS USED TO MAKE SKIS OUT OF BARREL-STAVES..
REALLY? SAY, THAT WAS PRETTY CLEVER! YES, SIR!
THEY REALLY DID THAT, HUH? WELL, I'LL BE! THAT WAS QUITE AN IDEA...

WHAT IN THE WORLD ARE BARREL-STAVES?
SCHULZ

SCHULZ

WITH CHARLIE BROWN, FLYING A KITE IS AN EMOTIONAL EXPERIENCE
SCHULZ

SCHULZ
US MAIL

GET UP THERE, YOU STUPID KITE!
YOU DIRTY KITE, GET UP THERE!! GET UP THERE!!
FLY, YOU STUPID KITE! FLY! FLY! FLY!
I'M ON YOUR SIDE CHARLIE BROWN
SCHULZ

HEY! COME QUICK! CHARLIE BROWN GOT HIS KITE UP!!!
IT'S FLYING!! IT'S FLYING!!
IT'S WAY UP IN THE... IN THE... IN THE OH OH
NEVER MIND
SCHULZ

SCHULZ
I SET THEM ALL FREE!

CLOUDS ARE VERY PECULIAR, LINUS.. SOMETIMES THEY SEEM TO FORM ACTUAL WORDS..
?
THOSE AREN'T CLOUDS... THAT'S SKY-WRITING!

CLOUDS ARE VERY PECULIAR, LINUS...SOMETIMES THEY SEEM TO FORM ACTUAL WORDS..
SCHULZ

YESTERDAY I FELT FINE..TODAY I'M ALL DEPRESSED...
DON'T WORRY ABOUT IT, CHARLIE BROWN...YOU'RE PROBABLY JUST UNSTABLE..
YOU'RE PROBABLY JUST UNSTABLE AND A LITTLE INCONSISTENT...
YOU'RE PROBABLY JUST UNSTABLE, A LITTLE INCONSISTENT AND SORT OF ERRATIC..

YOU'RE PROBABLY JUST UNSTABLE, A LITTLE INCONSISTENT, SORT OF ERRATIC AND..
GOOD GRIEF!
SCHULZ

THIS SOUNDS LIKE A GOOD MOVIE, "I WAS A TEEN-AGE WAR-MONGER".
OR HOW ABOUT THIS ONE, "I WAS A TEEN-AGE CAMEL DRIVER"?
WHICH ONE WOULD YOU LIKE TO SEE?
I DON'T KNOW...
IT'S DIFFICULT TO MAKE A DECISION WHEN YOU HAVE A CHOICE BETWEEN TWO SUCH OBVIOUSLY FINE PICTURES!
SCHULZ

BZZZZ
ZZZZZ
TWACK!
DEADLY!
SCHULZ

YOU NEED TO BE MORE FIRM, CHARLIE BROWN!
IF YOU WANT TO GO ALONG WITH THE CROWD, GO ALONG WITH THE CROWD!
BE LIKE THE WILLOW TREE... STAND UP, AND BEND WHICHEVER WAY THE WIND BLOWS!!
TAKE MY ADVICE, CHARLIE BROWN... STICK UP FOR YOUR RIGHT TO BE WISHY-WASHY!!!
SCHULZ

LOOK HERE, LUCY.. I DON'T LIKE ALL THIS TALK ABOUT ME BEING 'WISHY-WASHY'...
WHO DO YOU LIKE BETTER, YOUR MOTHER OR YOUR FATHER?
WELL, I.... I...
WISHY-WASHY!!!
SCHULZ

YOU KNOW WHAT OUR TEAM LACKED LAST YEAR?
IT LACKED ORGANIZATION! WELL, THIS YEAR IT'S GOING TO BE DIFFERENT!
I'VE WRITTEN DOWN THE NAME OF EACH PLAYER AND WHAT POSITION HE PLAYS, AND I'VE ATTACHED THE PAPERS TO A CLIP-BOARD...
IF THAT ISN'T ORGANIZATION, I DON'T KNOW WHAT IS!
SCHULZ

LUCY, HOW WOULD YOU LIKE TO PLAY SECOND BASE?
NOT ON YOUR LIFE!! I'VE GOT TOO MUCH PRIDE!
WELL, WHAT IN THE WORLD IS WRONG WITH SECOND BASE?
SECOND BASE? OH, PARDON ME...I THOUGHT YOU SAID "SECOND FIDDLE"!
SCHULZ

THUMP
I THINK I'VE FOUND A GOOD MAN FOR SHORTSTOP!
SCHULZ

A PITCHER AND HIS CATCHER NEED A GOOD SET OF SIGNALS...
ONE FINGER WILL MEAN A HIGH BALL...
TWO FINGERS WILL MEAN A LOW BALL...
AND THREE FINGERS WILL MEAN THE BROAD AREA IN-BETWEEN!
SCHULZ

HAVE YOU SEEN MY BAT, LINUS?
LUCY BORROWED IT...SHE SAID SHE NEEDED SOME BATTING PRACTICE..

I'VE BEEN HITTING A FEW ROCKS..
SCHULZ

WHAT LEAGUE ARE WE IN, CHARLIE BROWN?
WELL, YOU'VE HEARD OF THE MAJOR LEAGUES, THE MINOR LEAGUES AND THE BUSH LEAGUES, HAVEN'T YOU?
OH, YES, I'VE HEARD OF THEM..
WELL, HAVE YOU HEARD OF THE "LITTLE LEAGUE"?

OH, YES..
WELL, WE'RE ABOUT THREE LEAGUES BELOW THAT!
SCHULZ

WHAT SORT OF GIRL WOULD YOU LIKE TO MARRY, SCHROEDER?
WELL, I'D LIKE HER TO HAVE BLONDE HAIR...AND HAVE AN EVEN DISPOSITION...
AND I THINK SHE SHOULD BE FOND OF CLASSICAL MUSIC..
STRIKE THREE!!!!
SCHULZ

!
I CAN'T STAND IT! OF ALL THE DUMB THINGS HE'S DONE...
OH, I CAN'T STAND IT!!
?
!
SCHULZ

"A BOOK OF VERSES UNDER-NEATH THE BOUGH.."
"A JUG OF WINE, A LOAF OF BREAD AND THOU.."
NO BLANKET?
SCHULZ

EVERYBODY'S GOT THOSE NEW PLASTIC INNER-TUBES..
EVERYBODY?
UH, HUH...EVERYBODY!
SCHULZ

I SORT OF ADMIRE THAT LINUS...
HE'S READ "CINDERELLA," "PINOCCHIO," "SNOW WHITE."... ALL OF THOSE BOOKS..
AND THAT ISN'T THE ONLY THING...

HE CAN ALSO DISCUSS THEM INTELLIGENTLY!
SCHULZ

THE WAY I SEE IT, "THE COW JUMPED OVER THE MOON" INDICATES A RISE IN FARM PRICES...
THE PART ABOUT THE DISH RUNNING AWAY WITH THE SPOON MUST REFER TO THE CONSUMER..
DO YOU AGREE WITH ME, CHARLIE BROWN?
I CAN'T SAY...
I DON'T PRETEND TO BE A STUDENT OF PROPHETIC LITERATURE!
SCHULZ

THIS "GOLDILOCKS AND THE THREE BEARS" IS A TREMENDOUS STORY!
HMM...OH,OH! WELL, WHAT DO YOU KNOW? MMMM....MMM...
OH, THIS IS GREAT STUFF, CHARLIE BROWN!
YOU'VE JUST GOT TO TAKE THE TIME TO READ IT CAREFULLY..
SCHULZ

YOU AND YOUR OL' BEETHOVEN! HE WASN'T SO GREAT!
WHAT DO YOU MEAN, HE WASN'T SO GREAT?
JUST WHAT I SAID!
HE WAS THE GREATEST COMPOSER WHO EVER LIVED!
PHOOEY!
HE NEVER GOT TO BE CLUB CHAMPION, DID HE? HUH? DID HE?!
SCHULZ

I THINK CHILDREN NEED MORE REAL UNDERSTANDING!
I SINCERELY DOUBT THAT MOST PARENTS EVER TRY TO UNDERSTAND THEIR CHILDREN..
WELL, I DON'T SEE HOW YOU CAN **EXPECT** THEM TO...
I KNOW FROM PERSONAL EXPERIENCE THAT IT WOULD TAKE A **GENIUS** TO UNDERSTAND **ME**!!
SCHULZ

DEAR PENCIL-PAL,
I HAVE BEEN WANTING TO WRITE TO YOU EVER SINCE CHRISTMAS.
DID YOU GET LOTS OF NICE PRESENTS? I GOT A SLED, A PAIR OF SWIMMING-FINS AND SOME
MOM, HOW MANY "G'S" IN "GOGGLES"?
TWO, DEAR..
AND SOME GGOGLES.
YOUR FRIEND,
CHARLIE BROWN
SCHULZ

SCHULZ
NOTHING LEFT BUT THE BARE BONES!

YOU KNOW WHAT?
NO, WHAT?
I ALMOST RAN AWAY FROM HOME YESTERDAY..
OH? WHAT HELD YOU BACK?
SCHULZ
MY BLANKET WAS IN THE WASH!

WHAT'S WRONG WITH WANTING TO BE LIKED?
I WANT PEOPLE TO LIKE ME! I WANT THEM TO SAY, "GEE, HERE COMES GOOD OL' CHARLIE BROWN.."
AND THEN I WANT THEM TO SAY, "GEE, IT SURE IS GOOD TO SEE YOU, CHARLIE BROWN!" NOW, WHAT'S SO WRONG ABOUT THAT?!
SCHULZ
HAVE YOU EVER NOTICED HOW BLUE THE SKY IS THIS TIME OF YEAR?

ARF
ARF
ARF
ARF ARF ARF
I GUESS I'D BETTER KEEP QUIET..
THERE'S NO SENSE IN DOING A LOT OF BARKING IF YOU DON'T REALLY HAVE ANYTHING TO SAY.
SCHULZ

THIS IS MENDELSSOHN'S 'SONGS WITHOUT WORDS'..
COULDN'T HE THINK OF ANY?
SCHULZ

LUCY'S LETTING ME CARRY HER ROLLER-SKATE KEY!

SCHULZ
HOW CAN YOU STAND HAVING HER BE SO GOOD TO YOU?!

SOME STARS ARE BIG, AND SOME STARS ARE LITTLE
YOU SURE KNOW A LOT ABOUT THE STARS, LUCY..
WELL, I'VE DONE QUITE A BIT OF STUDYING...
ONE OF MY BEST SUBJECTS IN SCHOOL WAS AGRICULTURE!
SCHULZ

DO YOU KNOW WHAT HOLDS THE STARS UP, LINUS?
WELL, I'M NOT SURE..
THUMB TACKS?
SCHULZ

I'D LIKE TO BE ONE OF THOSE CAMPUS DOGS..
ALL THOSE SORORITY GIRLS PATTING YOU ON THE HEAD AND HUGGING YOU...
I CAN SEE ME NOW...
BIG MAN ON THE CAMPUS!
SCHULZ

"BIG MAN ON THE CAMPUS.." GOOD GRIEF!

IF YOU WERE **REALLY** THE BIG MAN ON THE CAMPUS, YOU WOULDN'T BE A SNOB, YOU'D BE **FRIENDLY**!

SCHULZ

SCHULZ

IT SAYS HERE THAT CHILDREN CANNOT CONCENTRATE PROPERLY..
IT SAYS THAT CHILDREN CANNOT KEEP THEIR MINDS FOCUSED ON ONE PROBLEM FOR ANY LENGTH OF TIME..
THAT'S THE MOST STUPID THING I'VE EVER HEARD!
SCHULZ

SCHULZ

I PUT MY TOOTH UNDER MY PILLOW LAST NIGHT, BUT ALL I GOT FOR IT WAS A DIME..
THAT'S NOT VERY MUCH, IS IT?
I'LL SAY IT ISN'T. NOT THESE DAYS...
STILL, I SUPPOSE I SHOULDN'T COMPLAIN..
AFTER ALL, THEY DON'T BRING A **THING** ON THE **OPEN MARKET**!
SCHULZ

I'M A GIANT!
GIANTS ARE THIRTY FEET TALL!
I'M A GIANT AMONG LESSER MEN!
SCHULZ

HI, CHARLIE BROWN!
THEY'RE HAVING A SALE DOWNTOWN ON HI-FI JUMP ROPES!
HOW CAN A JUMP ROPE BE HI-FI?
SCHULZ

IT'S DISGUSTING, THAT'S WHAT IT IS!
WHAT'S DISGUSTING?
DID YOU EVER STOP TO CONSIDER ALL THE GERMS YOU PICK UP DRAGGING THAT STUPID BLANKET AROUND?
GERMS?
...SO I PICK UP A FEW GERMS ALONG THE WAY...WHAT'S THE DIFFERENCE?
SCHULZ
THEY'RE ON THAT END AND I'M ON THIS END!

I'M GOING TO TRY TO GIVE UP THIS BLANKET, CHARLIE BROWN..
I WANT YOU TO TAKE CARE OF IT FOR ME, BUT NO MATTER HOW MUCH I PLEAD, DON'T GIVE IT BACK TO ME!
GOOD GRIEF...I CAN'T DO IT...I THINK I'VE CHANGED MY MIND... PLEASE GIVE IT BACK..
OKAY, HERE!
YOU'RE WEAKER THAN I AM!!!
SCHULZ

LOOK CHARLIE BROWN..YOU'VE GOT TO HELP ME BREAK THIS BLANKET HABIT...
YOU HANG ONTO IT FOR ME, BUT DON'T GIVE IT TO ME EVEN IF I BEG YOU FOR IT! NO MATTER WHAT I TELL YOU, DON'T GIVE IT BACK TO ME!!
SCHULZ
I THINK I'VE CHANGED MY MIND...I WANT IT.
ALL RIGHT.. HERE..

NO NO NO NO
SIGH

THERE'S NO USE KIDDING MYSELF
WITHOUT THIS BLANKET I'D CRACK LIKE A PIECE OF OLD BAMBOO!
BESIDES, THIS BLANKET OFFERS ME WONDERFUL OPPORTUNITIES TO...
CLOMP!
SCHULZ
....TRAVEL!

LIKE BIRDS?
SCHULZ

I'M GOING DOWN TO THE PARK, AND I'M GOING TO WALK CLEAR AROUND IT..
WELL, HAVE A GOOD TIME..
THANK YOU...
ONE THING ABOUT "PIG-PEN"... HE'LL NEVER HAVE ANY TROUBLE FINDING HIS WAY HOME!
SCHULZ

YOU CAN'T BELIEVE ANYBODY THESE DAYS!
I'M GETTING SO I DON'T TRUST **ANYBODY**!!
THE ONLY PERSON IN THIS WORLD WHOM I REALLY TRUST IS CHARLIE BROWN..
AND I DON'T EVEN TRUST HIM!!!
SCHULZ

HERE'S YOUR COAT, CHARLIE BROWN!
AND HERE'S YOUR CAP! NOW, GO ON HOME! GET OUT OF HERE!
SCHULZ
YOU DON'T LIKE ME, DO YOU?!

I'VE GOT SOMETHING FOR YOU, CHARLIE BROWN..
THIS SHOULD BE A BIG HELP TO YOU DURING THE COMING YEAR...I'VE MADE UP A LIST OF ALL YOUR FAULTS!
ONCE I GOT GOING IT WAS HARD TO KNOW WHERE TO STOP
SCHULZ

HERE, CHARLIE BROWN... I'VE GOT ANOTHER LIST FOR YOU..
ANOTHER LIST?! GOOD GRIEF, YOU GAVE ME A LIST OF ALL MY FAULTS YESTERDAY!
OH, THESE AREN'T FAULTS, CHARLIE BROWN..
THESE ARE SHORTCOMINGS!
SCHULZ